Russia Dies Laughing proves that a strong sense of humour survives even in oppressive societies. Just as Londoners joked their way through the blitz so, it seems, the citizens of Soviet Russia are joking their way through the desert of post-war Communism.

There are more than 200 jokes in this collection which, one hopes, may one day find its way to the three friends in Leningrad – A.N., R.N. and K.S. – whose skill as raconteurs led to the marathon joke-telling session on which it is based.

The jokes range from the political (Brezhnev, Krushchev and Comrade Lenin are among the targets) to the scatological and, along the way, we find that the Russians too have their bored wives and sexually incompetent husbands, their rude waiters, off-hand doctors and precocious children. It is both funny and revealing to see where our experiences overlap.

# Russia Dies Laughing

## Jokes from Soviet Russia

———

*Compiled and classified by*

A.N., R.N., and K.S.

*Edited and introduced by*

Z. Dolgopolova

*Illustrated by* JAK

London
UNWIN PAPERBACKS
Boston          Sydney

First published in Great Britain by André Deutsch Limited 1982
First published by Unwin Paperbacks 1983
Reprinted 1983

**UNWIN® PAPERBACKS**
**40 Museum Street, London WC1A 1LU, UK**

Unwin Paperbacks
Park Lane, Hemel Hempstead, Herts HP2 4TE, UK

George Allen & Unwin Australia Pty Ltd
8 Napier Street, North Sydney, NSW 2060, Australia

ISBN 0 04 827085 7

Printed in Great Britain
by Cox and Wyman Ltd, Reading

# Contents

# Introduction

During a break in a summit meeting in Helsinki, President Carter asked Brezhnev whether he collected stories against himself.

'I certainly do,' replied Brezhnev.

'Do you have many?' asked Carter.

'Two camps full,' said Brezhnev.

The above is only a joke. Brezhnev does not yet put people in prison for telling jokes and Krushchev before him set free many a Soviet citizen whose fondness for such stories had earned him five or ten years 'recognition' in Stalin's corrective labour camps.

The threat of outright liquidation removed, Russians create an endless stream of jokes about their rigidly regimented private and public lives, so much so that the form has become something of a cult.

The funny story or *anecdot* mocks the stifling seriousness of the official order, where even what is not forbidden is not permitted. It creates its own anti-world, in which the forbidden becomes permissible.

The normal order is turned upside down: in place of party meetings there is a brothel, in place of fiery slogans — four-letter words. In this world everyone says and does the unexpected: Kosygin would not mind emigrating from the

USSR, Brezhnev wishes Russia's capitalist food suppliers long life, and Marx begs the proletariat of the world to forgive him. The *anecdot* strips its heroes of decorations and uniforms, despatches them to the bath-house, the lavatory, the drinking hall — where all are equal and all speak the naked truth.

Despite the liberties it takes with officially serious and incontestible matters, it pretends to nothing but laughter, which suppresses fear and provokes thought.

This book was conceived around the kitchen table of a tiny Russian kitchen, the standard gathering place for groups of friends. More serious discussion dissolved into a marathon of joke-telling, in which the three R's — an architect, an artist and a writer — easily outshone the rest for their inexhaustible store of jokes and their skill as raconteurs.

The tape recording surviving this marathon lacks the mimicry and gestures of the live performance, the written record lacks the vividness of colloquial speech and the classification sacrifices the spontaneity of recall. What is left relies heavily on the skill of the translator and the quickness of the reader.

Z. Dolgopolova
*Victoria, Australia*

THE PARTY MAKES A SOLEMN PROMISE
THAT THE NEXT GENERATION OF
SOVIET PEOPLE WILL LIVE UNDER COM-
MUNISM.
Slogan of the Central Committee of the Communist
Party after the 22nd Party Congress.

Krushchev was furious with the joke tellers: 'It is a disgrace! Jokes and then more jokes! Who makes them up? Bring me just one joke writer!'

They bring a joke writer to him. The joke writer pauses in the doorway of Krushchev's home and looks around.

'What are you looking for?' Krushchev asks him.

'I'm just looking. I see you don't live too badly.'

'Well what of it? In twenty years we will have Communism and everybody will live like this!' says Krushchev.

'Oh-h-h!' the joke writer exclaims joyously. 'A new joke!'

# On Politics and Politicians

— What's the difference between a misfortune and a disaster?
— A great difference. For example, a goat is walking across a bridge, loses its footing and falls into the river. That's a misfortune but not a disaster. But if an aeroplane carrying the whole of the government crashes and everybody is killed, that's a disaster but no misfortune.

## The Leaders and the People

— How's life?
— Like a bus trip, one's driving and the rest shaking.

*

Kennedy comes to God and says: 'Tell me, God, how many years before my people will be happy?'

'Fifty years,' replies God.

Kennedy weeps and leaves.

De Gaulle comes to God and says: 'Tell me, God, how many years before my people will be happy?'

'A hundred years,' replies God.

De Gaulle weeps and leaves.

Krushchev comes to God and says: 'Tell me, God, how many years before my people will be happy?'

God weeps and leaves.

*

In Stalinist Moscow a man is running along the street shouting: 'The whole world is suffering because of one man! One man!'

He is seized and dispatched to the KGB.

There, he is taken to the interrogator's room.

'What were you shouting in the streets?' asks the interrogator.

'I was shouting that the whole world suffers because of one man.'

'And who did you have in mind?' The interrogator's eyes narrow.

'What do you mean, who?' The man is astonished. 'Hitler, naturally.'

'Ah-h-h . . .' smiles the interrogator. 'In that case you are free to leave.'

The man walks the length of the room, reaches the door, opens it and suddenly stops and turns around to face the interrogator.

'Excuse me, but who did *you* have in mind?'

*

Every morning a man would come up to the newspaper stand, and buy a copy of *Pravda*, look at the front page and then toss it angrily into the near-by bin.

The newspaper-seller was intrigued.

'Excuse me,' he said to the man, 'Every morning you buy a copy of *Pravda* from me and chuck it in the bin without even opening it. What do you buy it for?'

'I'm only interested in the front page,' replied the man. 'I'm looking out for a death notice.'

'But you don't get death notices on the front page,' said the newspaper-seller, taken aback.

'I assure you, the death notice I'm looking for will be on the front page.'

\*

Stalin was dead.

The Soviet nation decided to get rid of him once and for all and bury him as far away as possible. They set up a special commission. The commission turned to the British government with the request that they make available a plot in a British cemetery.

'Well,' replies the British government, 'we do already have Karl Marx in England . . . Two such great masters in the one cemetery . . . That would be overdoing it a bit . . .'

So they tried the Germans.

'Well, we would bury him here,' reply the Germans, 'but Hitler is already buried here. Two such great tyrants in the one country . . .'

Suddenly there arrived a telegram from Tel Aviv: 'In view of the fact that Stalin did not block the creation of the state of Israel, we agree to bury him here.'

'No way,' said the members of the commission in sudden panic. 'No way. After all they had a resurrection there . . .'

\*

Nehru arrived in Moscow on an official visit. It was seven a.m. He went out on to the balcony of his official residence. In the street below he could see trams and trolley-buses jammed full of people.

'Who are they all?' asked Nehru.

'Russia's masters,' replied Krushchev.

Eleven a.m.

Nehru went out on to the balcony again. He saw a number of black limousines driving by.

'Who are they?' asked Nehru.

'That's us!' announced Krushchev proudly. 'The servants of the people.'

\*

A man ran through the streets of Moscow shouting: 'Krushchev is a swine!'

He was seized and given twenty-one years: one year for defamation, and twenty years for leaking state secrets.

\*

Krushchev arrived in Paris. He went into a brothel\* and asked the madam: 'How much for a room?'

'Depends on the room,' she replied. 'There are 500 franc rooms, 100 franc rooms, 50 franc rooms and 1 franc rooms.'

'Give me a 1 franc room,' said Krushchev.

He was shown to a room. He sat there for ten minutes, but

---

\* In one of many such efforts to debunk a party leader this story dispatches him to a brothel instead of a party congress.

nobody came. For twenty . . . still nobody. For thirty . . . still nothing happened.

Nikita Sergeevich was outraged and rang for the madam. The madam appeared.

'This is an outrage!' shouted Krushchev. 'I've been waiting here for half an hour and no one has shown up!'

'I beg your pardon, monsieur,' replied the madam, 'but this room is self-service . . .'

\*

A man turned up in Moscow who, even blind-fold, could tell from a skull who it had belonged to.

The authorities got interested. They decided to test him out.

They blindfolded him and brought in the skull of Karl Marx. The man felt the skull carefully all over. 'A theoretician,' he pronounced. 'A thinker.'

Next they brought in Lenin's skull.

The man turned it this way and that. 'A pragmatist with a theoretical streak,' he asserted.

The authorities were astounded. They led in Krushchev.

The man fingered Krushchev's bald head for several minutes. 'It's clearly an arse,' he said, 'but I can't for the life of me find the hole!'

\*

— What would happen if Stalin rose from the dead?
— Krushchev would outstrip America.\*

\*

Brezhnev had a nightmare: a Czech was sitting in Red Square eating matzos — with chopsticks.

\*

\* 'We'll catch up with and outstrip America,' was one of Krushchev's most frequent exhortations

. . . Yesterday in Moscow an attempt was made on Comrade Brezhnev's life by an unidentified assailant. The bullet penetrated the bullet-proof car window, hit Comrade Brezhnev on the forehead, ricocheted and killed the driver.

*Tass communiqué*

\*

Brezhnev was being conducted around hell. 'Well,' the demons say to him, 'choose yourself a torment.'

They pass sinners sizzling in giant frying pans. 'What about that one?' ask the demons.

'N-n-no. . .' says Brezhnev, trembling. 'Not that one.'

They go on and see sinners being beaten with burning brands.

'What about that?' ask the demons.

'N-n-no. . .' says Brezhnev, trembling. 'Not that.'

They go further and suddenly they see Krushchev in bed with Brigitte Bardot.

'That's the one I want,' cries Brezhnev.

'Ha ha ha!' laugh the demons. 'That's Brigitte Bardot's torment.'

\*

President Ford and Brezhnev agreed to draw caricatures of each other.

'Only, no pornography, please,' says Brezhnev.

Ford agrees.

They do their drawings. Brezhnev hands his to Ford and Ford hands his to Brezhnev.

Ford has drawn Brezhnev as a strapping peasant with two

huge breasts and a snake around his neck.

'What are those?' asks Brezhnev.

'Well the snake is Cuba and the two breasts are the two halves of the world. With one you're feeding Africa and with the other Asia.'

'And what do I feed my own people with?' Brezhnev couldn't restrain himself.

'But, Mr Brezhnev, you said no pornography!'

Kosygin is talking to Brezhnev.

'Why don't you want to open up the borders?' asks Kosygin.

'Well, I would,' says Brezhnev, 'only I'm afraid everybody would rush out. We would be the only two left.'

Kosygin looks at Brezhnev in astonishment.

'You and who else?'

*

### Morning

Leonid Ilyich Brezhnev went out on to the balcony.

'Hello, Leonid Ilyich, good morning,' he heard a voice say.

Brezhnev wondered who could be addressing him so respectfully. He looked right, then left, but saw only the sun.

'Was that you who said hello to me?' Brezhnev asked the sun.

'Yes, that's right,' replied the sun.

'Well then, hello, hello,' said Brezhnev, gratified that even the sun looked up to him.

*Midday*

Again Brezhnev went out on to the balcony.

'Good day, Leonid Ilyich,' the sun greeted him respectfully.

'And good day to you, too,' replied Brezhnev condescendingly.

*Evening*

Once more Brezhnev went out on to the balcony and waited for the sun to greet him. But the sun was silent.

'Why don't you greet me?' asked Brezhnev, frowning.

'Get fucked,' said the sun. 'I'm in the West now!'

## On Communism and Soviet Rule

— What sort of a job should you take, so as never to be unemployed?
— Climb up on the Kremlin wall and watch for the approach of Communism.

\*

Brezhnev asked the Computer Centre to calculate how far they were from Communism. The scientists fed all the data into the computer and waited.

A day passed, another, a third . . . and finally the computer disgorged its answer on perforated tape: 18 kilometres.

The scientists were astonished. It must be a mistake. The programme would have to be repeated.

They repeated it but again they got the same reply.

The institute's old janitor suddenly hit on the explanation:

'Listen, friends, there's no mistake, it's perfectly correct. Comrade Brezhnev told us that each Five-Year Plan would bring us one step closer to Communism.'

\*

A commission visited a school to investigate the inculcation of patriotism among its pupils.

'Hymie,' asked a member of the commission, 'who is your father?'

'My father is the Soviet Union,' replied Hymie.

'Good boy! And who is your mother?'

'The Communist Party,' replied Hymie.

'Good boy! And what do you want to be when you grow up?'

'An orphan.'

\*

An old woman asks her granddaughter: 'Granddaughter, please explain Communism to me. How will people live under it? They probably teach you all about it in school.'

'Of course they do, Granny. When Communism comes, the shops will be full — there'll be butter, and meat, and sausage . . . you'll be able to go and buy anything you want . . .'

'Ah!' exclaimed the old woman joyously. 'Just like under the tsar!'

Two old Muscovites, Haim and Abraham, were walking along a street in the centre of Moscow.

'Do you remember, Haim, how before the revolution there used to be a shop on this corner and there were always barrels of sturgeon outside?' asked Abraham.

'Do I remember? Of course I remember! How could I forget? And what about on this corner? Do you remember? There used to be booths where they sold fresh caviar!'

'But listen, Haim, the only thing I can't understand is what did anyone have against it?'

\*

An old Leningrader received news from abroad that he was heir to a huge fortune. The KGB were on his doorstep immediately demanding that he transfer his inheritance to the USSR. The Leningrader held out for a long time, but then agreed — on one condition.*

'I'll transfer my fortune to the USSR on condition that for one day all the shops in Leningrad will give everything away free.'

The authorities thought about this, and since the inheritance was vast, they decided to agree.

The next day all the shops in Leningrad gave their goods away free. There was pandemonium — people climbing over one another, children crushed. The hospitals and soon the morgues too were filled to overflowing . . .

'See what you've done,' the authorities say to the man. 'What on earth did you want this to happen for?'

'I'm an old man,' replies the Leningrader, 'and before I die I badly wanted to see what Communism would be like.'

\*

* In fact, any inheritance received by a Soviet citizen from abroad is confiscated by the State, willy nilly. In return, the State issues the 'donor' with an insignificant percentage of the inheritance in roubles.

Haim and Abe meet again after a long separation.

'Ah!' cries Abe. 'How are you? How is your family? How are your children? I remember, you had three sons. They must be grown up?'

'Yes,' says Haim, 'they are. One lives in Moscow, he's building Communism. The second lives in Warsaw, he's building Communism too. The other one lives in Israel.'

'Is he building Communism too?'

'Are you out of your mind? In his own country?'

*

A Soviet citizen had died.

'Well,' he was asked in heaven, 'which would you rather, the communist heaven or the capitalist hell?'

The Soviet citizen smiled. At least he was allowed a free choice. And of course he chose the capitalist hell.

A year went by and the citizen applied to God to be transferred to the communist heaven.

'By all means,' said God, 'you may transfer.'

The citizen moved to the communist heaven where the inhabitants crowded round him and asked: 'Well, what is it like in the capitalist hell?'

'It's exactly the same as here as far as I can see,' says the citizen. 'Even the work is the same. They're pumping water too.'

'How many hours do they work?'

'The same as you do.'

'Then why did you want to come here? It seems there's no difference between here and there.'

'Oh-h-h . . .' says the citizen, 'there's a very big difference. There you have to work from eight a.m. to eight p.m. whereas here first they organize a party meeting, then a conference, then they hound you to another meeting, then it's smoke time and by then the pump could have broken down . . .'

*

Brezhnev's mother came to visit her son.

'This is my house,' said Brezhnev, showing her around. 'And this is my car. And that's my swimming pool. And this' — he

shows her some photographs — 'is my second house. And this is my aeroplane. And this is my villa on the Black Sea. And this is my yacht.'

His mother gasps in wonder.

'You do live well, Lyonechka,' she says. 'But I am nervous for you. What if the Bolsheviks* come back?'

\*

\* 'Steal their loot!' (Bolshevik cry of 1917).

— How do you relate to the Soviet government?
— Like a wife: part habit, part fear and wish to God I had a
  different one.

\*

An old Jew made an illegal attempt to flee the Soviet Union.
He was caught on the border, and interrogated by the KGB.

'Citizen Rabinovich, what made you decide to try to escape?'
asked the interrogator.

'I had two reasons,' replied Rabinovich. 'Firstly, if the Soviet
government collapses, everyone will blame us, that is, the Jews
. . .'

'Don't talk such rot!' shouted the interrogator. 'The Soviet
government is stronger than ever! It will never collapse!'

'That's my other reason . . .'

\*

An international flight. A stewardess prepares to make an
announcement: 'Ladies and gentlemen, we are extremely
fortunate. We have Jesus Christ on the plane with us. He is
about to come into the cabin and grant each passenger one
wish.'

A minute later Jesus Christ enters the cabin. He goes up to
the first passenger.

'What is your wish?' Jesus asks him.

The passenger, who turns out to be a rabid fascist, replies: 'I
wish that all communists would disappear from the face of the
earth.'

'Very well,' says Jesus and calmly proceeds to the next
passenger.

The next passenger is a rabid communist.

'What is your wish?' Jesus asks him.

'I wish that all fascists would be got rid of,' says the communist.

'Very well,' replies Jesus and moves on to the third. The third is a Jew.

'What is your wish?' Jesus asks him.

'Mr Jesus,' says the Jew, 'may I ask you one question?'

'By all means,' replies Jesus.

'Are you really going to do everything these gentlemen ask?'

'Of course,' replies Jesus. 'I am God.'

'Mm . . .' says the Jew. 'In that case I would just like a cup of coffee.'

## On Propaganda

— How can you ensure that your refrigerator is always full of food?
— Plug it into Radio Moscow.

\*

Two Muscovites meet.

'How's life?'

'Fantastic.'

'Do you read the papers?'

'Of course! How else would I know?'

\*

Brezhnev and Napoleon meet in the next world.

'Oh-h-h, if only we'd had such a brilliant commander as yourself in the Soviet Union instead of Stalin,' Brezhnev says to Napoleon, 'then we wouldn't have allowed Hitler to cross our threshold.'

'And if I had newspapers like your *Pravda*,' says Napoleon, 'not a soul would have heard about Waterloo.'

Stalin, Krushchev and Brezhnev are travelling in a train.
The train breaks down.
'Fix it!' orders Stalin.
They repair it but still the train doesn't move.
'Shoot everyone!' orders Stalin.
They shoot everyone but still the train doesn't budge.
Stalin dies.
'Rehabilitate everyone!' orders Krushchev.
They are rehabilitated, but still the train won't go.
Krushchev is removed.
'Close the curtains,' orders Brezhnev, 'and pretend we're moving!'

*

A Soviet made car — a Zaporozhets — was travelling along the Chicago-New York freeway. After a while it broke down. A Buick stopped, and took it on tow. Just at this moment a Ford overtook the Buick. Automatically, the driver of the Buick accelerated. The two cars raced at eighty, ninety, then a hundred miles an hour . . . The Zaporozhets bobbed along behind on the tow rope jerkily sounding its horn at the Buick to make it stop, because the Zaporozhets was all but falling apart.

The next morning there was a paragraph in the Soviet papers: 'Yesterday a Buick and a Ford were racing at a hundred miles an hour on the Chicago-New York freeway. Just behind them raced a Soviet Zaporozhets blowing its horn furiously, to get them to give way.'

The Kremlin organized a race between Brezhnev and Nixon. Nixon was first to the finishing line, and Brezhnev second.

Next morning the Tass communiqué read: Yesterday a race took place in the Kremlin. Comrade Brezhnev gained second place, and Nixon came second last.

## *Free Speech and Democracy*

— What does two times two make?
— Whatever the Party says.

During a break in a summit meeting in Helsinki, President Carter asked Brezhnev whether he collected stories against himself.

'I certainly do,' replied Brezhnev.

'Do you have many?' asked Carter.

'Two camps full,' said Brezhnev.

At the 20th Party Congress as Krushchev recounted the evils perpetrated by Stalin, a voice came from the hall: 'And where were you then?'

'Would the man who asked that question stand up,' said Krushchev.

The questioner took fright and did not stand.

'That's where we were, too!' replied Krushchev.

*

Two sparrows meet on the Soviet border. One is flying from France to the Soviet Union, the other from the Soviet Union to France.

'What do you want to come here for?' the Soviet sparrow asks the French sparrow.

'Well, you see,' replies the French sparrow, 'I'm hungry. In France nobody spills grain on the roads, there are no holes in the barns, and I'm starving. Now I've heard that in the Soviet Union there are holes in the barns and they spill grain on the roads . . .'

'That's true,' says the Soviet sparrow. 'There *are* holes in the barns and there *is* grain on the road . . .'

'Then why are you flying in our direction?'

'Well, how can I explain it,' replies the Soviet sparrow sadly. 'There is grain on the roads and you won't die of hunger . . . but I'm bursting to be allowed to sing . . .'

\*

A guest lecturer was giving a lecture about plenty and the ever-growing prosperity of the Soviet people.

In the back row Rabinovich puts up his hand.

'Comrade lecturer, what you say is very interesting but where has all the meat gone then?'

The next day the guest lecturer was giving another lecture on plenty and the ever-growing prosperity of the Soviet people.

In the back row Haimovich puts up his hand.

'Comrade lecturer, I don't want to know what has happened to the meat but can you tell us what has happened to Rabinovich?'

\*

An American and a Russian were arguing about which had the more perfect democracy.

'We have absolute democracy,' says the American. 'If I want to, I can go to the White House and shout "Remove Nixon!"'

'Ha!' replies the Russian. 'What's so special about that. If I want to, I too can go to the Kremlin and shout "Remove Nixon!"'

\*

A Western newspaper reported that dentists in the Soviet Union extract teeth through the patient's nose.

The paper was flooded with letters from readers asking how they had found this out.

The newspaper replied: 'Dentists are forced to extract their patients' teeth through the nose, because in the Soviet Union nobody dare open his mouth.'

\*

A certain Moscow family, fond of telling jokes, owned a parrot. One day it disappeared. They hunted high and low, but it was nowhere to be found. Without wasting any time the parrot's owner rushed to the KGB.

'Why come to us?' they asked. 'We haven't got your parrot, no one's brought it here.'

'Never mind, Comrade Commander, it's bound to be brought in soon and I just wanted to tell you that I don't share its opinions.'

\*

Rabinovich was sent abroad on official business. He arrived in Poland and telegraphed his factory in Moscow:

LONG LIVE FREE WARSAW! RABINOVICH

He arrived in Czechoslovakia and telegraphed:

LONG LIVE FREE PRAGUE! RABINOVICH

He arrived in Paris and telegraphed:

LONG LIVE PARIS! FREE RABINOVICH

## *Under Lock and Key*

A KGB interrogator asks a suspect: 'Which of my eyes is artificial? If you guess right I'll let you go.'

'The left one,' replies the suspect.

'How did you guess?' marvels the interrogator.

'It has a kindly look about it.'

*

The year is 1937. There are mass arrests in the Soviet Union. People live in fear, every night expecting to be carted away . . .

One night there is a loud knock at the door of a certain house. The tenants cower in silence, afraid to answer it. The knocking continues, getting louder and louder. The tenants go on pretending to be asleep. Finally someone begins to break the door down. At this, one tenant thinks to himself: 'I'm an old man, I've got to die soon anyway. What am I afraid of? I'll open up to them.' He gets out of bed and goes to the door. A minute later he rushes back shouting for joy. 'Comrades, comrades, get up! It's only a fire . . .'

*

Conversation in a prison cell:

'What are you in for?' one prisoner asks the other.

'For nothing. This is the third time I've landed in a bit of trouble. The first time they put me in was in 1924 just after Lenin died. I was working in a factory then. Some commissar came to read us a lecture. "The death of Comrade Lenin," he said, "it's a national grief. All the factories have closed and there are a hundred thousand wreaths . . ." And I said to him: "Comrade Commissar, for that money, never mind Lenin, you could bury the whole party . . ." They gave me ten years!

'Well I served my ten years, came out and got another job in a factory. Then Stalin died, there was a change of government and Beria was shot. And as soon as this was reported in the newspapers the party organizer said to me: "Ivanov, go and take down that bandit's portrait." But we had an awful lot of portraits hanging up in the factory. And I asked, "Which one?" That put me in the second time.

'For a second time I came out and thought to myself, "This time I won't be caught saying a word . . . I won't get involved in politics again." And there I was on the First of May marching with the other workers from our factory. They shoved a pole with Krushchev's portrait into my hand and said to carry it. Well, they told me to carry it, so I carried it. But behind me there was this drunk who kept treading on my heels. I said to him once, "Stop treading on my feet." I told him a second time, then when he kept on I turned around and said, "If you tread on my feet once more you bastard I'll beat shit out of you with the clown on this stick . . ." I got three years . . .'

*

A Russian and a Jew were sentenced to death. The prison governor granted each of them a final wish.

'What is yours?' he asks the Russian.

'I want to make confession.'

'Very well,' says the governor. 'A priest will be brought.'

He turns to the Jew. 'And what is yours?'

'Before I die I want to eat a bowl of strawberries and cream.'

The prison governor is astonished. 'Where will I find strawberries in Siberia in winter?'

'There's no hurry, Comrade Governor. I can wait.'

— What's the tallest building in any Soviet city?
— The one you can see Siberia from.*

## *On the International Wavelength*

*A new Soviet initiative on disarmament . . .*

A provincial is combing Moscow for a sewing machine. He tries shop after shop — no luck. At last he comes to one where the salesgirl says: 'Are you crazy? A sewing machine in Moscow? You'd have a much better chance of finding one in Tula, they make them there.'

'But I come from Tula. There aren't any sewing machines in the shops there.'

'Well, then, go to the factory which makes them and get one there.'

* There is a KGB office in every city of the USSR.

'But I work in the factory.'

'Then knock off the spare parts and put them together at home.'

'I've tried that three times already.'

'So, what happened? Didn't you know how?'

'Of course I knew how to put them together. But every time I did it I got a machine gun.'*

\*

* Every Soviet industrial complex houses at least one secret workshop which produces arms. This hidden industry does not show up in the Soviet military budget as published in the newspapers. It is, however, vast and would equal about half of the official military budget.

*News from our brother countries . . .*

HUNGARY

A Hungarian whispers: 'Please God let Hungary be invaded three times by the Chinese.'

'Janos, what are you saying? Why do you want them to invade us?'

'Well, to invade us three times, they'll have to cross the Soviet Union six times.'

POLAND

A Pole comes into a Warsaw bank.

'I have a hundred zlotys,' says the Pole. 'I can't decide what would be the safest thing to do with them.'

'Put them in the bank,' says the bank clerk.

'But what if the bank crashes?' says the Pole.

'If the bank crashes, then the bank administration guarantees to refund your money,' replies the clerk.

'Well, what if the administration goes bust?'

'Then the Polish Ministry of Finance guarantees to refund your money.'

'Well, what if the Ministry of Finance goes bust?'

'Then the Polish government guarantees to refund your money.'

'Well, what if the Polish government goes bankrupt?'

'Well, in that case the friendly Soviet Union guarantees the return of your money.'

'And what if the Soviet Union goes bankrupt?'

'You bastard, you don't mean to say that you'd begrudge a hundred zlotys for that?'

CZECHOSLOVAKIA

The Czech government approached the government of the USSR with a request for help in setting up a Ministry for the Navy. The Soviet government asked the Czech government why it needed a Ministry for the Navy when it had no sea. To which they received the reply: 'Why do you have a Ministry for Culture?'

\*

*Between friends* . . .

A Soviet diplomatic car was travelling along the highway in a friendly African state when it hit a mud patch and got bogged down. The Russian ambassador emerged from the car and asked the citizens of the friendly state for help. The citizens agreed to help drag the car out.

'Pu-u-ush!' they shouted, standing stock still.

'Pu-u-ull!' they shouted, standing stock still.

'Why on earth are you yelling instead of pushing?' asked the ambassador.

'Oh, we're following the example of our Soviet brother!'

\*

*An important tactical decision* . . .

Nasser phones his commanders on the Sinai front.

'Why aren't you attacking?'

'Mr President, we are employing the tactics of the great Russian General Kutuzov\* — we are waiting for the snow to fall.'

\*

---

\* The Russian general who, with the help of the Russian winter, defeated Napoleon.

*The great victory for Soviet diplomacy at the Helsinki conference*

President Ford, Giscard d'Estaing, Harold Wilson and Brezhnev assembled for a conference. After days of conferring they decided to take a break — they would go to India to hunt elephants.

Well, they did, and the very first day, towards nightfall, they caught an elephant. Now, what were they to do with it? They decided to tie it to a tree and agreed to take turns in guarding it.

The first on guard was President Ford. He stood guard for two hours, woke Giscard, then went to sleep. Giscard stood guard for two hours, woke Wilson, then went to sleep. Wilson stood guard for two hours, woke Brezhnev, then went to sleep. Brezhnev went to sleep too.

In the morning they woke up and there was no elephant.

'Where's the elephant?' they ask Brezhnev.

'What elephant?'

'What do you mean "What elephant"?' The others are indignant. 'Did we come to India to hunt elephants?'

'We did.'

'Did we catch an elephant?'

'We did.'

'Did we tie it to a tree?'

'We did.'

'Did we agree to take turns guarding it?'

'We did.'

'Did Ford stand guard?'

'He did.'

'Did he hand the elephant over to Giscard?'

'He did.'

'Did Giscard stand guard?'

'He did.'

'Did he hand the elephant over to Wilson?'

'He did.'

'Did Wilson stand guard?'

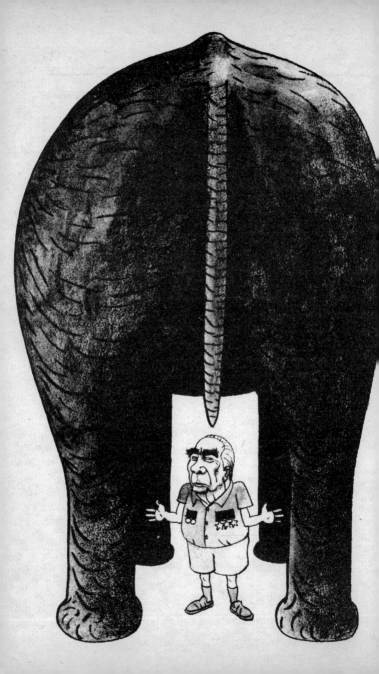

'He did.'
'Did he hand the elephant over to you?'
'He did.'
'Then, where *is* the elephant?'
'What elephant?'

\*

*We answer readers' queries . . .*
— Why has the Soviet government recently been exiling dissidents to Western Europe?
— As part of turning Western Europe into western Siberia.

— Will there be a war?
— No, there won't be a war. But there will be such a struggle for peace that no stone will be left standing.

— What would you get if you tore the head off the dove of peace?
— The atom bomb.

# We Are Catching Up with America

— How's life?
— Like on a boat. It makes you sick but you can't get off.

## On Abundance

A conversation in a restaurant in the Republic: 'Do you have any pilau?'
'Yes, we do. But we don't at the moment.'
'Do you have any shashlik?'
'Yes, but not at the moment.'
'Do you have any buttermilk?'
'Yes, but not at the moment.'
'Do you have any tea?'
'Yes, I'll bring it straight away.'

*

Nehru arrived in Moscow on official business and was making a tour of the Soviet capital. He saw a queue and walked up to it.

'What are you queuing for?' he asked.

'They're giving out sugar,' replied the citizens.

'Well, well!' Nehru is surprised. 'Here they give out sugar whereas at home we usually sell it.'

He walked further. There was another queue.

'What's going on here?' Nehru asked.

'They're throwing out shoes!'

Nehru looked at the shoes, twirled a pair in his hands: 'No wonder,' he said. 'In India we throw out shoes like this too.'

\*

A man is running through the streets of Moscow with a chamber-pot on his head.

'What are you doing with that pot on your head?' a passer-by asks him.

'They say that you can get shit down town.'

\*

A commission visited a Moscow maternity hospital. The babies were being weighed. It turned out that all the Jewish new-born infants weighed more than the Russian. The Russian mothers were outraged. 'Don't worry ladies,' the commission soothed them. 'After all, we are preparing them for export.'

## Our Achievements

The passenger cabin of an aircraft. A voice announces over the intercom: 'Ladies and Gentlemen, we welcome you on board the world's first fully automated intercontinental airliner which was built by Soviet aeronautical engineers.

'We will be flying at ten thousand metres with a cruising speed of five thousand kilometres an hour. There are no pilots on board the aircraft and no service personnel. It is entirely controlled by electronics. All the instruments are working normally . . . working normally . . . working normally . . . working normally . . .'

— What would happen if Leningrad underwent as severe an earthquake as the one in Tashkent? *
— You'd be left with St Petersburg.

Nixon arrived in Moscow. He was met by Krushchev who showed him over the capital, particularly the new construction areas.

'What are those things sticking out over there?' asked Nixon, pointing at the roof tops.

* There was a severe earthquake in Tashkent in 1966. The first buildings to crash were buildings of the Soviet period.

'What do you mean, what are they?' Krushchev is astounded. 'They're television aerials.'

'That's great!' says Nixon. 'You haven't only caught up with us, there are some areas in which you have outstripped us!'

'What areas?' asks Krushchev over-joyed.

'Well, we've never ever thought of installing television sets in pigsties.'

*

'Did you hear that the director of our match factory was awarded the Order of Lenin?'

'What for?'

'A spy tried to set fire to an ordnance factory with our matches and he couldn't . . .'

## Service with a Smile . ..

— When are grey hairs particularly obvious?
— When they're floating in tomato soup.

*

A man is sitting in a restaurant eating a thirty-copeck bowl of soup. Suddenly he fishes an iron nut out of the bowl. The indignant customer demands to see the head cook. Out comes the head cook.

'What's this?' asks the man angrily, indicating the nut.

'An iron nut,' replies the head cook.

'Why is there an iron nut in the soup?' fumes the customer.

'What do you expect for thirty-copecks,' says the head cook, 'a whole tractor?'

\*

Three men were sitting at a restaurant table. Up came the waiter.

'I'll have a steak, medium rare, and boiled potatoes,' says the first man.

The waiter writes down the order.

'And I'll have a veal cutlet with fried potatoes,' says the second man.

The waiter writes it down.

'And for me, please, roast beef with baked potato,' says the third.

The waiter turns towards the kitchen: 'Vanya,' he shouts to the chef, 'three meats!'

\*

A man enters a restaurant and says to the waitress: 'A steak and a kind word, love.'

The waitress brings him the steak and turns to go.

'What about the kind word?' says the man playfully.

The waitress bends down to him and whispers: 'Don't eat it, the meat's off.'

### Life on the Collective Farm

On the left a sickle
On the right a hammer
That's our Soviet emblem.
So whether you reap the corn
Or strike the anvil
Either way
You get fuck all.

\*

The Minister for Agriculture was on an inspection tour of the collective farms. He arrived at one run by a Comrade Ivanov.

'What do you feed the hens on?' the minister asks him.

'We buy in grain,' replies Ivanov.

The minister was angry.

'How dare you when there's a grain shortage in the country? Fire him!' the minister ordered.

They fired him.

The minister arrived at the next collective farm, administered by a Ukrainian, Galushko.

'What do you feed the hens on?' the minister asks him.

'We buy in corn,' says Galushko.

The minister flew into a rage.

'How dare you! We are buying that corn from Canada with gold. Have him charged!' orders the minister.

They have him charged.

The minister arrived at the next collective farm, administered by Comrade Rabinovich.

'What do you feed the hens on?' asks the minister.

'Comrade Minister,' replies Rabinovich, 'we give them a rouble each and tell them to feed themselves.'

\*

Roosevelt, Churchill and Stalin went to inspect a collective farm. They had to cross over a bridge. But there was a cow standing on it.

Churchill got out of the car and advanced on the cow, intending to drive it away.

'Moo-o-oo . . .' went the cow and lowered her horns at Churchill. Churchill backed off.

Up came Roosevelt.

'Moo-o-oo . . .' went the cow and lowered her horns at him too. Roosevelt backed off.

Up came Stalin and whispered something to the cow. The cow raised its tail in fright and took off.

'What did you say to her, Joseph?' asked Churchill and Roosevelt.

'I told her that if she didn't get out of the way I would put her in a collective farm.'

\*

In Kazakhstan at a meeting of collective farm workers a lecturer was delivering a lecture on agriculture:

'Comrades, the year before last was a bad harvest because . . .'

A voice from the hall breaks in:

'They say that the Jews . . .'

'What have the Jews got to do with it!' interrupts the lecturer. 'The rainfall the year before last was two hundred millimetres below average . . .'

A lecturer was delivering a lecture to a group of collective farm workers in Georgia.

'Comrades, last year was a poor harvest . . .'

A voice from the hall:

'They say that the Jews . . .'

'What have the Jews got to do with it! The rainfall last year was two hundred millimetres above average.'

A lecturer was giving a lecture to collective farm workers in the Ukraine.

'Comrades, we're expecting a poor harvest this year because . . .'

A voice from the hall:

'They say that the Jews . . .'

'Why does everybody keep on about the Jews!' The lecturer is getting angry.

'Well, they say the Jews pay nine hundred roubles to be allowed to leave the USSR. Is that true?'

'Yes, it's true!'

'Well, that's what I mean,' the voice continues. 'Maybe instead of the crops we should be cultivating the Jews!'

## *. . . and Other Trifles*

An American spy is dropped by parachute on to Soviet territory. He immediately decides to give himself up. He makes it to a town, finds the appropriate organization and goes up to the doorman:

'Listen, friend, I'm an American spy and I want to give myself up. Who should I see?'

'Second Floor, Room 218,' replies the doorman.

The spy gets to Room 218.

'I'm an American spy. I want to give myself up.'

'What's your area, sabotage, terrorism or ideology?'

'Sabotage,' replies the spy.

'Then you've come to the wrong place. Go to Room 613 on the sixth floor.'

The spy gets to Room 613.

I'm an American spy specializing in sabotage. I want to give myself up.'

'Did you specialize in transport or industrial targets?'

'Transport,' replies the spy.

'Well that's the seventh floor, Room 742.'

The spy gets to Room 742.

'I'm an American spy specializing in the sabotage of transport. I wish to give myself up.'

'What kind of transport, road or railway?'

'Railway,' replies the spy.

'Then you've come to the wrong place. Room 936, ninth floor.'

The spy gets to Room 936.

'I'm an American spy specializing in the sabotage of rail transport. I wish to give myself up.'

'Look here, Comrade, don't you see that it's six o'clock? We've finished interviewing for today. Come back tomorrow . . .'

*

A man comes to see his friend, a minister, and says: 'I need your help to get a job because I haven't any qualifications.'

'Are you a Party member?' asks the minister.

'Of course,' replies his friend.

'Okay, then,' says the minister, 'I could make you my deputy. You would be getting ten thousand roubles a month!'

'Oh, no,' says the man, 'I'd rather something less grand.'

'Very well then,' says the minister, 'I can appoint you director of a large factory, two thousand roubles a month . . .'

'No,' says his friend again. 'That's still far too grand. I was thinking of around a hundred roubles a month . . . as an engineer perhaps . . .'

'I'm sorry, says the minister, 'I can't get you a job as an engineer. You need qualifications for that . . .'

# *East and West*

One Englishman makes a gentleman.
Two Englishmen makes a bet.
Three Englishmen make a parliament.

One Frenchman makes a lady's man.
Two Frenchmen make a duel.
Three Frenchmen make a Paris commune.

One Jew makes a merchant.
Two Jews makes a chess tournament.
Three Jews make an orchestra.

One Russian makes a drunkard.
Two Russians make a fight.
Three Russians make the beginnings of a Party organization.

*A husband comes back unexpectedly.*
French wife:   Jacques, move over, my husband's back.
German wife:  Hans! You're two minutes early!
Jewish wife:    Haim! Is that you? Then who's this with me?
Russian wife:  (falling on her knees) Ivan, hit me, but not in the face.

## Foreigners on Russians

An Englishman, a Frenchman and an American were arguing about the nationality of Adam and Eve.

'They must have been English,' declares the Englishman. 'Only a gentleman would share his last apple with a woman.'

'They were undoubtedly French,' says the Frenchman. 'Who else could seduce a woman so easily?'

'I think they were Russian,' says the American. 'After all, who else could walk around stark naked, feed on one apple between the two of them and think they were in paradise?'

\*

There were two brothers, an American and a Russian.

The American was jobless and hungry. But he had an idea: he went to the gates of the White House, sat on the ground outside and began eating hay. Kennedy saw him there and asked: 'What are you eating hay for?'

'Because I'm hungry and I haven't a job.'

Kennedy was outraged and ordered that he be fed and given some money.

'What else would you like?'

'A ticket to Russia to visit my brother.'

Kennedy made the arrangements and the American flew to Russia where he found that his brother was starving too. The American burst out laughing and said: 'Brother, I can give you a good piece of advice. Go to the Kremlin, sit on the ground by the gates and eat hay. Out will come Krushchev who will be angry to see you in such a state and give you everything you need.'

And that's what the Russian brother did. He sat down by the Kremlin gates and began eating hay. Out came Krushchev and saw him there.

'What are you eating hay for?' he asked.

'Because I'm hungry and I haven't any money.'

'You're a fool!' says Krushchev. 'It's summer now, you should be eating grass and leaving the hay for winter.'

\*

A Soviet architect was on a trip abroad. A foreign architect invited him to his home. He showed his Soviet guest around the house.

'This is the hall,' he explained, 'and this is the sitting room. This is my study, those are the children's bedrooms, this is the main bedroom and this is a spare room for visitors. Then there are the kitchen, the dining room, the two bathrooms, the lavatory . . .'

'It's a very good layout,' says the Soviet guest.

'What sort of layouts do you have?'

'Us? We have much the same, only without the partitions . . .'

\*

A Russian spy was known to be in London. Scotland Yard was beside itself, but couldn't find him. Eventually, they turned to Sherlock Holmes.

'How many public lavatories are there in London?' asked Sherlock Holmes.

'Five hundred,' he was told.

'Then, give me five hundred detectives.'

He was given five hundred detectives.

Towards evening the spy was caught.

'How did you do it?' The police were astonished.

'Simple,' replied Sherlock Holmes. 'I put a detective outside every public lavatory and told them that if they saw a man coming out still doing up his fly, that would be him.'

\*

A foreigner was wandering around Moscow one night. He approached a policeman and asked:

'Tell me please, where is the nearest bar?'

'The nearest bar? In Helsinki.'

\*

England received an order from the Soviet Union for one hundred thousand condoms. The dimensions were unusual: length — half a metre, diameter — ten centimetres.

The English turned to Churchill: What should they do about it?

Churchill thought for a minute and then ordered: 'Make them! Make them and stamp them: Made in England, medium size.'

\*

The war was over! The allied armies were celebrating! The admiral of the American fleet invited on board the Russian and English admirals. After the banquet they began talking about courage.

'Our sailors are afraid of nothing,' said the American admiral, 'they are prepared to go through fire and water.'

They decided to put this to the test. The American admiral summoned a sailor and ordered him: 'Shin up that forty-metre mast and dive into the sea.'

The sailor reddened with rage, but saluted, climbed up the mast and jumped. They dragged him out of the water barely alive.

'Fantastic!' said the Soviet admiral. 'Gentlemen, I insist that tomorrow you be my guests at dinner.'

The next day the same company gathered on board a Soviet ship. After the banquet the Soviet admiral summoned a sailor and ordered him: 'Shin up that forty-metre mast and dive head-first on to the deck.'

The sailor turned pale, saluted, climbed the mast and flung himself on to the deck. There was nothing left of him.

'Well, gentlemen,' said the English admiral, 'it must be my turn now. I invite you to dine on board my ship tomorrow.'

After the banquet the English admiral summoned a sailor and said: 'Would you mind awfully shinnying up that forty-metre mast and diving down the funnel.'

The sailor turned green with fury.

'Yes I would, sir, and get fucked, sir!'

'The English admiral shrugged his shoulders and turned to his colleagues: 'You see, gentlemen, there is more than one kind of courage.'

## Russians on Foreigners

A Frenchman is visiting a woman. She is waiting for him in bed. The Frenchman is overcome by passion. He tears off his beret and tosses it out of the open window. He throws off his coat and flings that out too. Now out of the window with his boots . . .

'Monsieur! What are you doing?' cries the woman.

'Don't worry, madame,' replies the Frenchman. 'By the time I'm finished it will all have gone out of fashion.'

\*

An Englishman goes into a tavern.

'Supper and a bottle of wine!' he orders.

The tavern keeper brings him the food and wine.

The Englishman eats his supper and says: 'It wouldn't be bad to have a woman now.'

'Second floor, third door on the left,' says the tavern keeper.

The Englishman goes up to the second floor.

A little while later he descends.

'Well, sir, how was it?' asks the tavern keeper.

'Oh, she wasn't bad, not bad at all,' says the Englishman, 'but a little cold . . .'

'Yes, she would be!' says the tavern keeper. 'She's been dead for two days . . .'

*

Churchill was sick in bed. A young adjutant was sent to amuse him.

'How old are you?' asks Churchill.

'Twenty-seven,' replies the adjutant.

'Are you married?'

'Yes, Mr Prime Minister.'

'Children?'

'Eight, sir.'

'How many?'

'Eight, sir.'

'Hmm . . .' mutters Churchill. 'How did you manage that . . . and you're still very young . . .'

'Well, you see, sir, I love my wife very much . . .'

'And I love this, young man,' says Churchill pointing to the cigar poking out of his mouth, 'but from time to time I do take it out . . .'

*

On the shore of the Indian Ocean a raggedy Indian fisherman lay dozing with a hat over his face. Beside him two fishing lines were stuck into the sand.

Up comes an American.

'What are you sleeping for?' says the American. 'You'd be better off catching fish.'

'What for?' asks the fisherman.

'What do you mean, what for? You'd catch some fish, you'd sell them and with the money you'd buy yourself a trawler. The trawler would catch even more fish. You'd sell it and buy yourself an even bigger boat. You'd catch still more fish. You'd sell it. Then you'd build yourself a fish processing factory . . . and get rich. And then you could lie on the beach and sleep.'

The fisherman pulled his hat even further down over his face.

'But that's what I'm doing now.'

*

The end of the Second World War. The allied armies meet on the Elbe. A Russian officer is lying in bed with an American woman. The American woman takes an orange from the table, peels it and places the peel neatly in a little jar.

'What do you collect orange peel for?' asks the Russian.

'We make fruit conserves from the peel and send them to Russia,' says the American woman.

An hour went by. They fucked, the Russian took off his French letter, folded it neatly and put it in his pocket.

'What do you collect used French letters for?' the American woman asks in amazement.

'We make them into chewing gum and send them to America.'

*

President Johnson was standing in the loo peeing. Beside him was Martin Luther King. Johnson took a sideways glance at King.

'Is it true,' asked Johnson, 'that all negroes have big pricks?'

'As you see,' replied King.

'I wonder how they get them?'

'Oh, it's simple,' replied King. 'Every night before I go to bed I whack my prick on the end of the bed. It strengthens it.'

The working day came to a close. Johnson went home, had dinner and went upstairs. His wife was waiting for him in bed. Johnson took off his trousers, went up to the head of the bed and began whipping his prick against it.

His wife stared at him in astonishment: 'Stop acting like a goddamn nigger and come to bed.'

*

The Pope was dying and his followers were given to believe that his life would be saved if he slept with a woman.

'That's impossible,' said the Pope. 'I am the Holy Father and cannot contravene God's law.'

They spent a long time trying to persuade him. 'It is in order to save your life, so that you can serve God further,' they argued. And at last the Pope agreed.

'All right,' he said, 'but the following conditions must be fulfilled. In the first place, the woman must be blind, so that she cannot see me.'

'We shall find a blind one,' they answered.

'In the second place, she must be deaf, so that she cannot hear my voice.'

'We shall find one who is deaf too,' they promised.

'Thirdly, she must be dumb, so that she cannot tell anyone what has taken place. And fourthly, she must have big tits . . .'

*

ISRAELI ARMY REGULATIONS:
1 When given the order to stand 'at ease' don't wave your arms about.
2 Don't talk on reconnaissance.
3 Don't twiddle your commander's buttons when he's speaking to you.
4 Don't give advice to the Commander in Chief.

A man went to visit a Bavarian friend and noticed that both his ears were bandaged.

'What's the matter with your ears?' he asked.

'Something very stupid happened,' replied the Bavarian. 'I was ironing some clothes and suddenly the phone rang. So instead of the receiver, I put the iron to my ear.'

'But what about the other ear?'

'Well, I had to ring the doctor.'

— How do you sink an Arab submarine?
— Knock on the hatch.

# *Jews and Anti-Semites*

Two drunks were walking down the street when towards them came a Jew. One drunk elbowed the other: 'Hey, Vanya, let's give this Yid a good going over, eh?'

'Well, we could,' replied the second, 'except that he looks bloody fit. What if he were to give us a good going over?'

'Vanya!' his friend was surprised. 'Why would he hit us?'

## *Anti-Semites on Jews*

'Haim, someone's fucking your wife on the woodpile.'
'Which woodpile? The one on the right or the one on the left?'
'The one on the left.'
'That's not my woodpile.'

*

Abraham is sitting in a tram when suddenly he sees Haim running along behind.

'Haim, what are you doing running after the tram?' yells Abraham.

'I'm saving three copecks,' replies Haim.

'You idiot!' shouts Abraham. 'You'd be better off running behind a taxi and saving three roubles.'

\*

An Orthodox priest, a Catholic priest and a rabbi were talking together.

'How much of the collection do you give God and how much do you keep for yourself?' the Catholic and the rabbi asked the Orthodox priest.

'I divide all the money coming into the Church into a big pile and a small pile; the big one is for God and the small one is for me,' says the Orthodox priest.

'Well,' says the Catholic priest, 'I divide the money into two even piles, one for God and one for me.'

'I put all the money on a tray and throw it up into the air,' says the rabbi. 'And what God wants God keeps.'

\*

A Russian, a Ukrainian and a Jew were travelling on a train. It was a long and boring journey.

'Let's have a game of cards,' says the Russian.

'But we haven't got any cards,' says the Ukrainian.

'Never mind,' says the Russian. 'Instead of cards we'll put out food. For example, a lump of lard can be the Queen of Hearts, half a litre of vodka the King of Clubs and so on.'

They began playing.

'Queen of Hearts,' declares the Ukrainian putting a lump of lard down on the table.

'King of Clubs,' says the Russian putting out a half litre.

'Nothing is trumps,' says the Jew, putting down nothing and collecting up the lard and the vodka.

\*

Krushchev summoned a Russian, a Ukrainian and a Jew.

'Comrades,' he says to them, 'the Central Committee has decreed that three men must be sent into space. You can name your own reward.'

The Russian thought for a bit and said: 'A hundred thousand roubles.'

The Ukrainian thought for a bit: 'Two hundred thousand roubles.'

The Jew thought for a bit: 'Nikita Sergeevich, I cannot diddle the Soviet State. Just like a taxi, twenty copecks a kilometre.'

\*

At an international conference, delegates were sitting at a long table drinking coffee when a fly landed in each delegate's cup.

The Englishman pushed his cup away.

The Frenchman extracted the fly, and drank his coffee.

The Arab ate the fly and drank the coffee.

The Jew collected up all the flies he could find and sold them to the Arab.

Revolution. A fully armed worker's division is marching through Petrograd. Haim and Abraham are standing by the window watching them.

'We will march bravely into battle . . .' sing the marchers.

Haim opens the window.

'And we'll follow you . . .' he joins in the refrain.

'And we shall die to a man . . .' continue the marchers.

Abraham slams the window shut:
'Die on your own . . .'

\*

— What's the difference between a Russian and a Jew?
— The Russian dies but doesn't surrender, whereas the
  Jew surrenders but doesn't die.

\*

To test the nutritional value of corn Krushchev summoned a
Russian, a Ukrainian and a Jew and ordered them to eat
nothing but corn for three months.

At the end of this period they were brought to Krushchev
again to be weighed. The Russian had lost twenty kilograms,
the Ukrainian ten, whereas the Jew had gained five.

Krushchev was overjoyed: 'Well, Comrade Rabinovich, tell
us how you did it!'

'Quite simple, Comrade Krushchev. I filtered the corn
through chickens.'

\*

Haim and Abraham are sitting on the loo having a crap.
'Haim,' asks Abraham, 'do you think this is physical or
mental work?'
'I think it must be mental,' replies Haim.
'Why?' asks Abraham.
'If it were physical I'd hire somebody to do it for me.'

\*

A conversation between Soviet Jews after the Six Day War:
'Haim! Did you hear how we beat us?'

\*

Delegates from several different countries are in an aeroplane.
Suddenly it begins to lose height. The captain emerges from his
cabin and says: 'Gentlemen, somebody will have to sacrifice
himself. The aeroplane is overloaded.'

The first to approach the hatch is a Frenchman: 'Long live
free France!' he shouts and jumps.

The second is an American: 'Long live free America!' he
shouts and jumps.

The third is a Jew: 'Long live free Israel!' he shouts and he
seizes an Arab and throws him out.

\*

Rabinovich arrives in Paris, finds the house he is looking for
and knocks on the door. It is opened by a very beautiful
woman.

'Good day,' says Rabinovich. 'Can I spend the night with
you?'

The woman is outraged.

'But, why not?' says Rabinovich soothingly. 'I will give you a
hundred pounds . . .'

The woman thinks; 'A hundred pounds is a lot of money . . .'

'Very well,' she agrees.

Rabinovich sleeps with her, gets up in the morning, gives
her the money and leaves. In the evening he comes back.

'Can I sleep with you one more night? I will give you another
hundred pounds.'

The woman hesitates.

'Very well,' she says, 'but this must be the last time.'

Rabinovich sleeps with her, gives her the money in the morning and leaves. In the evening he is back again.

'No, not again,' says the woman, 'that's enough . . .'

'This is the last night,' says Rabinovich. 'I'll give you another hundred pounds.'

'Very well,' she finally agrees, 'but this night really will be the last . . .'

Rabinovich sleeps with her, gets up in the morning and gives her the money.

'Tell me,' the woman says to him as he is leaving. 'Where are you from?'

'From Tel Aviv,' says Rabinovich.

'I've got an aunt living there, a Madam Nekrich,' says the woman. 'Do you know anyone of that name?'

'Well, yes, . . .' says Rabinovich. 'It was she who asked me to give you the three hundred pounds.'

\*

There was a shipwreck. Everybody drowned with the exception of two Jews. Once on shore they were besieged by journalists:

'Mr Rabinovich! Mr Khaimovich! How did you manage to survive?'

'Survive?' Rabinovich and Khaimovich are perplexed. 'Why, what happened?'

'What do you mean what happened? The ship sank. Everyone was drowned. How on earth did you manage to swim ashore?'

'Swim ashore? We've no idea. Khaimovich and I were just talking.'\*

\*

---

\* The stereotype Jew waves his arms about as he talks.

Haim and Abraham meet.

'How's life?' asks Abraham.

'Not bad,' replies Haim.

'What are you doing for a living?' asks Abraham.

'I'm working as a secretary to a lord,' replies Haim.

'Why, that's terrific!'

'Yes, yes, it's all right, except that the lord is paying attention to my wife.'

'Haim, that's terrible!'

'Yes, it's bad,' agreed Haim, 'but then I'm paying attention to his wife.'

'Well, then everything's all right.'

'Yes, everything's all right, only the lord is sleeping with my wife.'

'Haim, that's shocking!'

'Yes, it's shocking, but then I'm sleeping with his wife.'

'Then it's not so bad.'

'It wouldn't be so bad, but he's made me seven kids.'

'Haim, that's a disaster!'

'Well, maybe it's not such a disaster. I've made him seven kids too.'

'Then you're quits.'

'Quits, you think! I've made him seven lords and he's made me seven Jews.'

\*

It was winter. A rumour went round town that there had been a meat delivery. A huge queue formed outside the butcher's shop.

One hour went by, two, three . . . Finally, at eleven o'clock, the shop door was opened, and the manager announced: 'Friends, we have meat, but not enough for everybody. Would all the Jews please leave.'

The Jews left. The queue was significantly reduced.

At one o'clock the door opened again: 'Friends, we have meat, but not enough for everybody. Would all non-party members please leave.' Again the queue was significantly reduced.

At three o'clock the door opened again: 'Friends, we have meat, but not enough for everybody. Would all those who didn't take part in the Great War of the Fatherland please leave.'

At five o'clock the door opened again: 'Friends, we have meat, but not enough for everybody. Would all those who didn't take part in the overthrow of Tsarism please leave.'

There were only three half frozen old men left.

At eight o'clock the door opened once more: 'Friends, there won't be any meat.'

The old men moved off home grumbling: 'The Jews always get the best of everything!'

## Jews on Anti-Semites

In Odessa the synagogue had been shut down. A deputation of Jews went to the authorities to ask why.

'We couldn't find a suitable rabbi,' replied the authorities.

'One knew the Talmud, but didn't know Marxism-Leninism; a second knew Marxism-Leninism, but didn't know the Talmud; and the third knew all three, but he was a Jew.'

*

A Russian and a Jew were travelling on a train. At lunchtime the Jew took out some sardines and the Russian some chicken. They began to eat.

'Tell me,' said the Russian, munching away, 'how is it that all you Jews are so clever?'

'How can I explain it,' replied the Jew. 'Well, take our lunch for example. You're eating chicken and I'm having sardines. Sardines are fish, fish contain phosphorus and phosphorus improves the brain . . .'

The Russian thought for a bit:

'Listen, how about swapping?'

They swapped. The Jew polished off the chicken and the Russian ate the sardines.

'Well, now what?' The Russian began thinking aloud. 'I've eaten the sardines and I'm still hungry.'

'Ah-h-h!' said the Jew. 'You can see that it's working already!'

*

A special commission was selecting new recruits for the police force. In came the first candidate.

'What do two two's make?' they asked him.

'Three,' replied the candidate.

'Think again,' said the members of the commission.

'Five,' replied the candidate.

'Think again.'

'Seven,' replied the candidate.

'You may go.'

The candidate left. The commission recorded: 'Not educated but resourceful. Passes.'

In came the second candidate.

'What do two two's make?'

'Five,' replied the candidate.

'Think again.'
'Five,' repeated the candidate.
'Think again.'
'Five!'
'You may go.'
The candidate left. The commission recorded: 'Not educated, but resolute. Passes.'
In came the next candidate.
'What do two two's make?'
'Four,' replied the candidate.
'Think again.'
'Four.'
'Think again!'
'Four.'
'You may go now.'
The candidate left. The commission recorded: 'Educated. Check out his nationality.'

*

— How can a Jew get accepted into the Communist Party?
— On the recommendation of two Arabs.

*

A Jewish family is leaving for Israel. The husband is packing portraits of the Soviet leaders in his suitcase.
'What are you doing that for?' asks his wife in astonishment. 'Why on earth would you want to take those swine with you?'
'But, that's just it!' says the husband. 'If I ever begin to feel nostalgic I'll look at these and think to myself, thank God I left!'

*

A certain inhabitant of Odessa used to receive regular parcels from Israel. This aroused the interest of the KGB. They called him in.

'What's your name?'

'Ivanov.'

'First names?'

'Ivan Ivanovich.'

'Are you a Jew then?' asked the KGB man.

'How could I be a Jew?'* exclaimed the man in astonishment.

'Then how come you are receiving parcels from Israel?'

'Ah-ah-h . . . that's an old story. During the German occupation I hid two Jews in my cellar. Well, the war ended, they survived, they went to Israel and now out of gratitude they send me parcels.'

'So, Comrade Ivanov, you think you can live the rest of your life at the expense of these two Jews?'

'Why at the expense of these two? I'm hiding two more right now.'


## Jews on Jews

— Who was the first to reach the North Pole?
— The icebergs.

*

Rabinovich was called in by the head of the personnel department:

'Comrade Rabinovich, why did you put down a lie on your form?'

---

* 'Ivan Ivanovich' sounds about as Jewish as 'John Smith'.

'Where?' Rabinovich was amazed.

'Here, where it says "Do you have any relatives abroad," you have replied "No". But you have a brother in Israel.'

'But it's me who is abroad. He is at home.'

\*

Nixon to Golda Meier: 'You have a fine people!'

'It's you that have a fine people,' replies Golda Meier. 'I have a country full of presidents.'

\*

A conversation between two inhabitants of Berdichev.\*

'Haim, where did you get such a good overcoat made, eh?'

'My uncle sent it to me from Paris.'

'From Paris? Where is this Paris?'

'Oh, it's a long way away, two thousand kilometres from here.'

'Well, how about that, in the back of beyond they are making clothes!'

\*

A caravan was travelling across the desert. The travellers were tormented by thirst. Suddenly they see a kiosk selling

---

\* A small town in the Ukraine with a large Jewish population.

lemonade. The caravan passes by. Only Rabinovich jumps off his camel and races up to the kiosk.

'Hey, are you really selling lemonade?' he asks the Jewish storeholder.

'I am,' replies the storeholder sadly.

'Then you must be a millionaire!' cries an excited Rabonovich.

'Millionaire indeed . . .' snorts the storeholder. 'On the contrary — a beggar . . . Nobody believes their eyes. They think it is a mirage.'

## On Emigration, Race and the Brotherhood of Nations

Haim asks Abraham:

'Do you know how many million Jews are living in the Soviet Union?'

'About three, I think, but if free immigration to Israel were permitted there would suddenly be thirty-three.'

*

Haim asks Abraham:

'What would you do if the Soviet borders were opened?'

'I'd shin up the nearest tree,' replies Abraham.

'Why?' asked an astonished Haim.

'You'd get killed in the crush.'

*

Rabinovich came to the visa department to apply for a visa to Israel.

'You are making a great mistake leaving the Soviet Union,' the official there told him. 'You know the old saying, it's always better where we're not.'

'You're absolutely right,' agrees Rabinovich. 'That's why I'm going somewhere you won't be.'

\*

An old Armenian, the father of a large family, was dying. He called together the whole family, beckoned his eldest son, whispered something in his ear and died.

'What did Father say to you?' asked the relatives.

'He said, "Save the Jews!" '

The family thought and thought about what these last words could mean. Finally the wisest of them hit on it.

'What our father was saying was this: save the Jews because when they're finished, we'll be the next!'

\*

I once went on holiday to the Caucasus with two friends. First we went to Armenia to see Mount Ararat. There we were, in the mountains, having set up our tent and lit a fire, when an Armenian arrived on horseback and said: 'You and you,' he indicated my friends, 'please come to the kolkhoz to a wedding . . .'

My friends were invited but I was not. Of course I was upset. That evening my friends went to the wedding and I stayed behind. Two hours had passed when I saw the same Armenian coming up the hill towards me. As he approached he said: 'Listen, my friend, please forgive me. I mistook you for a Georgian. Let us go to the wedding . . .'

Well, after leaving Armenia we went to Tbilisi in Georgia. I was walking along the street there when I saw two Georgians having a fight. I interfered to separate them and for my pains got my face smashed in. We all were taken to the police station. The police demanded our passports. The Georgian who had beaten me up looked at my passport and gasped: 'I'm terribly sorry my friend,' he said, 'I thought you were an Armenian.'

After these two incidents I joyfully set off home to Kiev, to my beloved anti-semites. [An eye witness account.]

# Student Life

A yoga student wants to rent a nail in a corridor. — *Small ad in Moscow newspaper.*\*

\*

The setting: a remote village in the North where there are no women. A prostitute arrives in town. Her rates are a rouble to put it in, another to take it out. A rouble to put it back in and another to take it back out.

A long queue formed outside her flat. In went the first customer, then the second, third, fourth and fifth. The sixth to go in was a student.

Ten minutes went by and the student still hadn't come out. Fifteen minutes, twenty minutes — still he wasn't out. The queue began to get restless: 'Is he a millionaire . . .?'

One of the men looked into the room and saw that the student was lying on the prostitute not moving.

\* The student housing problem in Moscow is so bad that if a student fails to get into a hostel, he is happy to be able to rent a corner of someone's room.

'What are you doing holding up the queue?' he shouted at him.

'Well, I'd be glad to get out of here,' replied the student, 'but I haven't got the second rouble . . .'

\*

A BROTHEL MADAM'S MONOLOGUE
'Oh dear, oh dear! What are things coming to? In the old days a gentleman would come in and ask for Marushka. You would send him Marushka and he was so polite. He'd kiss her hand . . . he'd take her away into a private room and order champagne . . . then he'd amuse himself with her so tenderly and afterwards wipe his prick with a fine lawn handkerchief and throw it under the bed. I used to make three thousand a year just on the handkerchiefs . . . Now what? In comes a drunk student bawling, "Let's have Marushka!" You give him Marushka and he has the gall to be dissatisfied: "Why is Marushka so cold!" And he wants you to put an electric blanket under her bum! Then he screws her until she's half dead and wipes his prick on the curtains. Just on curtains I lose three thousand a year . . .'

\*

An expedition of scientists from Moscow got lost in an African jungle and fell into the hands of cannibals. They were brought before the chief.

'This one into the pot, that one into the pot,' said the chief. 'But leave this one alone: We studied together at Moscow University.'

## Some Questions and Answers

— Who took the first step towards building Communism in Russia — scientists or laymen?
— Laymen. Scientists would have tried it out first on dogs.

— Is it possible to set up Communism in France?
— Yes, it's possible, but it would be a pity.

— Why, in the last half century, has there not appeared one work of literature to equal *War and Peace*?
— Many writers consider that they could easily write another *War and Peace,* but they just don't have the time.

— Who were the first Marxist disciples of Hegel?
— Woodchucks. They peck around in Hegel's manure for a grain of reason.

— What is philosophy?
— Philosophy is something you can spend a long time chewing and never swallow.

— What is the difference between a student and a machine?
— There hasn't been a machine invented yet that can do nothing.

— For what achievement were the Moscow archeologists awarded the Lenin prize?
— For digging out the prehistoric mine shaft where Nikita Sergeevich Krushchev worked.*

— What's the lightest thing on earth?
— The penis. It rises at a mere thought.
— And what's the heaviest?
— The same thing. If it doesn't want to, a crane couldn't get it up.

— What's the difference between a sputnik and a mini skirt?
— A sputnik is maximum expense and minimum information whereas the mini skirt is minimum expense and maximum information.

* 'I, like you, am a working man. My working life began down a mine shaft . . .' From Krushchev's autobiography.

— Is it true that the Soviet Union is superior to the capitalist world in everything?
— Of course it's true. For example a Soviet dwarf is two centimetres taller than a capitalist dwarf.

# War Games

The commander returned from leave.

'Did anything happen while I was away?' he asked the soldier on duty.

'No, nothing at all,' replied the soldier. 'Except that the regimental dog had three puppies.'

'Oh, that's nothing,' said the commander.

'That's true,' went on the soldier. 'But a couple of men had a fight on account of those puppies.'

'Is that all?'

'Not quite,' replied the soldier. 'One shot the other and then hid in the ammunition store.'

'That's bad,' said the commander.

'It was bad. We had to storm the store to get him out.'

'Well, did you get him?'

'Of course we did, but the store exploded. And the regiment was blown up.'

*

An intercontinental nuclear missile control centre. A drunken soldier is dusting the missile control panel. Puffing and panting,

an enraged general rushes into the room: 'What are you doing, you son of a bitch?' he shouts.

'I'm dusting,' hiccups the soldier drunkenly.

'Well, where the hell has England gone?'

\*

A colonel was standing at the door to the barracks. Up came a drunk soldier. The soldier was seeing double, even treble.

'Comrade colonels,' barked the soldier, 'may I get past?'

'Okay,' hiccups the colonel, 'but go one at a time . . .'

\*

A lance corporal was giving a lesson in general knowledge to a class of privates.

'Well, it's like this,' said the lance corporal didactically. 'Water boils at ninety degrees.'

In the back row a soldier wearing glasses put up his hand.

'Yes?' said the lance corporal.

The soldier got up.

'Excuse me, sir, but water boils at a hundred degrees.'

The lance corporal looked annoyed.

'Well, we have got an educated lot here,' he grumbled, 'a whole crowd of four-eyes . . .'

He opened the textbook and began to search through it, muttering as he did so: 'Smart arses . . . the educated . . ,'

He found the place and looked up at the soldier in amazement.

'Well, can you beat it! You're right! It is a hundred. And ninety, that's a right angle . . .'

\*

Pushkin was prancing around St Petersburg on horseback.\* The envious were making fun of him:

'Pushkin rides a horse like a captain sails a ship!'

Pushkin flips up the horse's tail:

'Gentlemen, I invite you into the captain's cabin . . .'

\*

One morning after a heavy night's drinking an officer woke up and noticed his orderly cleaning his tunic.

'Oh, Vanya,' said the officer, 'did we get pissed last night!

\*Pushkin never served in any armed force, but he liked riding.

And there was one real pig there who was sick all over my tunic.'

'You're absolutely right,' said the orderly, 'he must have been a real pig, because he shat in your pants as well.'

\*

It was bath day for the soldiers. A change of underwear was announced:

'Hut 2 to change underwear with Hut 6 . . .'

\*

A soldier had his cock torn off at the front. The doctors worried about what they could do for the poor fellow and decided to make him a button-on one out of plastic. And so that it would be just like a real one, before each use he was to fill it with milk. A year passed, another and a third . . .

And suddenly the invalid's wife was pregnant!

. . . and gave birth to — three kilograms of butter.

\*

A Soviet guerrilla was being sent behind enemy lines. He was given a brief: to board a certain aeroplane that would take him to point M. There he was to jump. His parachute would open and when he landed he would find a car waiting to take him where he had to go.

When, the aeroplane reached point M the guerrilla jumped. He pulled the ring but the parachute didn't open: 'As usual,' thought the guerrilla. 'Wherever you go, the same old Soviet balls-up. I bet the car won't even be waiting when I get there . . .'

# Of Men and Women

A Georgian is making love to his bride but can't effect penetration. He tries and tries until he's half dead with exhaustion and his cock is raw. Finally he makes it . . .

'Phew,' he says, wiping the sweat from his face. 'I didn't know you were still a virgin . . .'

'Are you joking?' replies the bride. 'Did no one ever tell you not to throw a woman on to the bed before she's had a chance to take off her tights?'

A new gadget entitled 'Woman substitute' appeared in the shops. A man bought one and took it home. There was a piece of rubber pipe sticking out of it. He shoved his prick in this, pressed the button and the gadget began to work. It pulled him off for five minutes, ten, fifteen, and still it hadn't stopped. The man was exhausted. He'd come twice, but he had no idea how to switch the gadget off. Somehow he managed to reach the telephone and phone the shop.

'Don't worry,' he was told. 'It's an automatic milking machine for cows. As soon as the bucket's full it will switch itself off.'

\*

Two girls were buying sausages.

'I'll have two sausages, please,' one of them said to the salesgirl and held out the money.

'I don't have any change,' said the salesgirl. 'Take three.'

'Okay,' said the girl, 'give me three.'

'What will we do with the third?' the friend asked in a whisper.

'Don't fuss,' replied the first, 'we'll eat that one.'

*

Madam Ivanova complained to the housing commission that she could no longer live in her room.

'Why not?' they asked her.

'Well, just opposite my window is the men's bath-house,' she said, 'and there are naked men wandering around all day.'

They decided to send a team to investigate.

The inspectors came and looked out of the window. They couldn't see a thing.

'Madam Ivanova, you can't see a thing from your window!'

'Can't you, indeed! You just climb up on the cupboard!'

*

Christ came to Moscow. The hotels were all full. There was nowhere for him to stay. So he went to the Bolshoi Theatre. There were a number of women standing around outside. One of them grabbed hold of him and took him home.

In the morning as they were getting up she asked him his name.

'Jesus Christ,' he replied.

'Is that so?' the woman shrugged it off. 'Well, Christ or no Christ, you're a god in bed!'

\*

A married man came to visit a prostitute.
She was already waiting for him in bed.
'I have enough of that at home!' shouted the man angrily. 'Get up, get dressed, and resist!'

An elegant couple was walking down the street when a pigeon flew overhead and dropped a message on the woman's shoulder.

'Oh!' shrieked the woman and turned to her companion. 'Have you got any paper?'

Her companion looked up at the sky in surprise: 'What am I supposed to do, fly after him?'

*

A man had come to Moscow on business. He was wandering around town searching for the Ministry he had to visit. He stopped a passerby.

'Listen, mate, whereabouts is the such-and-such Ministry?'

'The Ministry? Ah, that's quite close. Let me see, straight ahead till you pass a pub, then you turn left and walk on till you come to a billiard shop on the corner; then you turn right — past a coffee bar — and you come to police station No. 46. But don't stop there, turn left again. A hundred yards ahead is the salami shop and right next door is your Ministry.'

The man puzzled over these directions for a minute or two, then gave up and stopped a woman.

'Excuse me, could you tell me where the such-and-such Ministry is?'

'Ah, the Ministry. That's very close. Straight ahead until you pass the stocking shop and then right next door is the haberdasher's and there you turn left. Then as you turn right again past the perfume shop, you'll see a beauty salon and opposite it a hairdresser. And then around the corner from the patisserie you'll find your Ministry.'

*

A woman was buying a broom in a store.

'Show me that one, please,' she says to the salesgirl.

The salesgirl brings it to her.

'No, that's not what I want,' says the woman.

'Perhaps this one?' suggests the salesgirl.

'No, not that one either.'

'What about this one then?' The girl keeps on trying.

After twenty minutes more of this the woman says: 'Very well, this one will do.'

'Madam,' says the harassed salesgirl, 'shall I wrap it for you or will you fly it home?'

*

An Armenian was standing in a shop when a woman with a beautiful bottom came in. 'Oh-h,' thought the Armenian, 'wouldn't it be marvellous to smack a bottom like that, mmm!'

He approached the woman and whispered: 'Listen, dear, let me slap you just once on the bum. I'll give you a hundred roubles.'

The woman thought for a bit — after all you don't find hundred-rouble notes lying in the street!

'All right,' she said, 'let's go outside and around the corner.'

They went round the corner and the Armenian started stroking her bottom, just stroking it . . .

'Well, get on with it,' said the woman crossly.

'Ah-h-h,' sighed the Armenian, 'if I had a hundred roubles I certainly would . . .'

# Out-Patients

'Doctor I can't pass water.'
'How old are you?'
'Seventy.'
'You've already passed it all.'

*

There was a queue outside the waiting-room of a doctor who specialized in instant cures.
In came a schoolboy.
'Doctor, I swallowed a pen.'
'Write in pencil. Next.'
In came a man holding his stomach.
'Doctor, my stomach aches.'
'Try rubbing your stomach on another stomach and it will get better fast. Next.'
In came a pregnant woman.
'Doctor, the baby's in the wrong position.'
'What's yur name?'
'Finkelstein.'
'He'll find a way out. Next . . .'

*

An Armenian* came to see the doctor, undid his trousers, produced his penis and laid it on the table.

'Have a look at it, doctor,' said the Armenian.

'What's the matter with it?' asked the doctor.

'Just look at it, look at it!' cried the Armenian.

'But what's the matter with it?' said the doctor again.

'Just look at it, doctor, isn't it beautiful!'

'Doctor, all you do is listen and tap the table with your pencil. You don't even ask me how I feel.'

'Well, how do you feel?'

'Don't ask!'

'What's the difference between a psychopath and a neurotic?'

'A psychopath knows for certain that two times two is five. Whereas the neurotic knows that two times two is four, but it bothers him.'

A commission of inquiry visited a lunatic asylum.

'How are you all getting on?' the members of the commission asked the patients. 'Are you happy with everything?'

'Very happy!' replied the inmates.

* To the Russian the Armenian is ⌐ model of virility.

'Do you behave well?' ask the members of the commission.

'Yes, we behave!' replied one of the inmates. 'As a reward for good behaviour they've built us a swimming pool with a diving platform, so that we can dive in to the swimming pool from the platform. And when we start behaving even better the doctor has promised that they'll fill the pool with water . . .'

\*

A patient was about to be released from a mental hospital.

'Well, Vanya,' says one of the doctors to him, 'you're cured. But let's examine you one last time before you go.

'Now I'm going to draw something for you. What does it represent?'

'It's obvious,' said Vanya. 'It's a room with a bed in it, and on the bed is a woman.'

'Well, what would you do if I were to give it to you?' asked the doctor.

'I would go into the room, fuck the woman on the bed and leave.'

'I see,' said the doctor. 'And what's this?'

'That's two rooms, two beds and two women. I would go into the first room and fuck the first woman, then I would go into the second room and fuck the second woman and then I'd leave.'

'And what's this?' asked the doctor.

'That's four rooms. I'd go into the first room and fuck with the first woman, then into the second room and fuck the second woman, then into the third room and fuck the third woman.

Then I'd go into the fourth room, fuck the fourth woman and leave.'

'And what's this then?' and the doctor drew another diagram.

Vanya looked at the doctor.
'Doctor, you're a sex maniac.'

An inmate in a lunatic asylum thought he was a grain of corn and was afraid of being eaten by hens.

At a routine meeting of the medical commission to discharge the patients that were considered cured, this patient was called in.

'How do you feel?' asked the doctor.

'Very well thank you,' said the patient.

'Do you know now what was the matter with you?'

'Of course I know, doctor. I thought I was a grain of corn.'

'And what do you think now?'

'Now I know that I'm not a grain of corn, I'm a person.'

'Wonderful!' said the doctor. 'Then we can discharge you and you can go home.'

The patient reached the door and turned around and faced the doctor: 'Doctor, I know I'm a man and not a grain of corn, but will the hens know that too?'

*

A man came to see the doctor.

'Doctor, you've got to help me. Every time I sleep with my

wife we have a child. I've made sixteen kids. What can I do, doctor?'

'My dear fellow, are you a child?' the doctor is astonished. 'You should use condoms.'

The man thanked the doctor for his advice and set off for home.

Some years passed and one day the doctor met his former patient on the street. Joyfully the patient rushed up to him.

'Thank you, my dear doctor, thank you for your advice.'

'So the condoms helped?' smiled the doctor.

'What do you mean, doctor helped? They helped all right! There's only one left.'

'One what left?' The doctor was nonplussed.

'What do you mean one what? There's only one child left.'

'Why, where are all the others?' asked the doctor in surprise.

'They're dead, doctor, they're dead!' cried the patient happily.

'What do you mean dead, what from?'

'From laughing, doctor. I took the condoms with buckwheat porridge and they came bubbling out of my arse, inflated and burst. And fifteen kids died laughing . . .'

# *Family Affairs*

### *Husbands and Wives*

Wife to husband: Close the curtains, or the man next door will
see me naked.
Husband to wife: If he sees you naked, he'll close the curtains.

*

A husband and wife got a divorce. They had a young
daughter. The husband had to pay his wife alimony until his
daughter turned eighteen.

On the eve of her eighteenth birthday the daughter came to
visit her father. He gave her the money and said maliciously:
'Tell your mother that this is the last payment.'

The daughter went home and gave her mother the message.

'Well you can tell your father,' said the mother, 'that he's not
your father.'

*

A wife is sitting in the bedroom with her lover when suddenly she hears her husband in the front room.

'Hide in the cupboard,' she whispers to her lover.

The lover slips into the cupboard. The husband comes in, takes off his jacket, opens the cupboard and notices a pair of shoes sticking out from under the dresses.

'And what's this?' the surprised husband asks.

'It's just us!' reply the shoes, amicably.

A man and his wife are making love. The husband asks his wife: 'Did I hurt you?'

'No, why?' asks his wife in surprise.

'You moved.'

A husband goes away on holiday.

Ten days later, he sends a telegram to his wife: 'Sell the wardrobe and send me the 100 roubles.'

Ten days later he telegraphs again: 'Sell the fridge and send me the 200 roubles.'

Ten days later: 'Sell the carpet and send me the 500.'

The husband returns home to an empty house. Everything has been sold.

'Okay,' says the wife, 'now you can stay at home and I'll have a holiday.'

Ten days go by. The wife sends a telegram: 'I'm sending you 500 roubles. Buy some furniture.'

*

Grandad and Granny were making love.
'You know Grandad,' says Granny, 'your prick's got fatter!'
'No it hasn't,' replies Grandad, 'I've just doubled it over.'


## *Parents and Children*


Little Petya asks his mother: 'Mummy, do dogs have spare parts?'

'How on earth could dogs have spare parts?' says his mother. 'After all, they are alive.'

'Well, then, why did Daddy tell Uncle Kolya that when you go on holiday, he's going to screw the arse off the bitch next door?'

\*


A little girl asks her mother: 'Where was I born?'
'You were born in Moscow, and I was born in Leningrad.'
'Well, where was Daddy born?'
'Daddy was born in Kiev.'
'How lucky we all met!'

\*


Sister to brother: 'Your prick is bigger than Dad's.'
'I know,' replies her brother. 'Mum says the same thing.'

\*

A passenger train pulled in to a station. Out of one compartment stepped a little boy with his mother and a chap covered in military decorations. They were met on the platform by the little boy's father.

'I'd like you to meet the co-occupant of our sleeper,' the wife said to her husband. 'He's a hero of the Soviet Union!'

'Some hero!' grumbled the little boy. 'He was afraid of going to bed without Mummy.'

*

A mother was putting her little son to bed.

'Go to bed, little one, go to bed . . . If you need anything in the night, just whisper "Mummy" and Daddy will come straight away.'

*

The maths teacher calls Petya up to the blackboard.

'Imagine that your father has borrowed a hundred roubles from a neighbour,' says the teacher, 'and has promised to give the money back in two weeks. The first week he gives back forty roubles. How much would he give back the second week?'

'None at all,' replies Petya.

'What do you mean, none at all?' the teacher asks, surprised. 'You weren't listening properly. Let me repeat: imagine that your father has borrowed a hundred roubles and promised to repay the money in two weeks. The first week he gives back forty roubles. How much would he give back the second week?'

'None at all!' repeats Petya.

'Oh, Petya,' the teacher is annoyed. 'You don't know the simplest arithmetic!'

'And you don't know my father . . .'

*

An ad in the paper: 'Flat to let to a family with no children.'

A man came to the flat and looked it over. He liked it, agreed to take it and the very next day he moved in. With him were a wife and seven children.

The enraged landlady exclaimed: 'Comrade, I warned you that the flat was to be let only to a family with no children.'

'Where do you see children?' said the man amazed. 'You call these children? They're not children, they're monsters!'

*

A young girl goes up to a coach in a sports' school and asks to be admitted to the gymnastics section.

'What can you do?' asks the coach. 'Show us.'

The girl undresses and places a large apple on the floor. She does the splits and the apple disappears.

The coach is amazed. 'With such talent you should go and work in the circus.'

'Oh, that's nothing!' The girl says airily. 'My mother can do it with a melon!'

### Just Children

A little boy, Petya, was standing at a front door trying to reach the doorbell. A policeman was passing by:

'What's the matter, little fellow, can't you reach it? Shall I help?'

The policeman lifts him up and gleefully Petya rings the bell.

'Now, mister,' says Petya, 'let's piss off.'

*

A group of children were taken on a picnic to the woods. A little girl ran off into the bushes to pee. She pulled up her dress, she pulled down her pants, squatted down and sat right on a prickle . . .

On the way back she saw a little boy peeing.

'Oh!' she said. 'That's a handy thing to take on a picnic.'

*

Teacher to pupil:

'Petya, why weren't you at school the day before yesterday?'

'Mother washed my underpants,' said Petya, 'and hung them up to dry, and I haven't got any others.'

'Well, why weren't you at school yesterday?'

'Well, I was coming to school yesterday, only when I was walking past your house, I saw your pants drying on the line and I thought you wouldn't be coming.'

# *Our Glorious Past!*

Karl Marx's address to the 23rd Congress of the
Communist Party of the Soviet Union:
'Workers of the world! Forgive me!'

## *Comrade Lenin*

A historic speech!

It was after work one evening. Yakov Mikhailovich Sverdlov*
dropped in to Vladimir Ilich Lenin's study.

'Vladimir Ilich, why don't we crack a bottle together?' said
Sverdlov.

'No, no and again no!' said Lenin. 'Absolutely not.'

'Come, Vladimir Ilich! Just one between the two of us . . . last
time we cracked two bottles between three and nothing very
terrible happened.'

* Sverdlov, Yakov Mikhailovich, (1885-1919), one of Lenin's comrades
  in arms.

'I like your "nothing happened"! You and Dzerzhinsky went off home to bed, whereas I climbed up on the roof of an armoured car and spouted such a load of bullshit . . .'*

\*

Vladimir Ilich Lenin was making a typically fiery speech. Looking up at him was a small Jew.

'Excuse me, Comrade Lenin, can I ask a question?' asked the little Jew.

'Of course, Comrade! Of course!' replied Vladimir Ilich.

'I don't suppose you could tell where you got such a fine waistcoat?'

'This one?'

Vladimir Ilich shoved his left thumb under his armpit, and flung his right arm forward in the direction of Finland:

'There!'

---

\* On 16 April 1917, on his return from exile in Switzerland, Lenin made an impromptu speech from the roof of an armoured car outside the Finland Station in Petrograd.

Lenin was cross with his wife: 'Nadenka, why are you going around in such a torn and dirty skirt?'

'Because I've nothing else to wear,' she replied.

'What do you mean nothing!' Lenin was indignant and opened the wardrobe.

'Look, there's a blue dress, a brown outfit, a leather jacket ... Hello, Comrade Dzerzhinsky* ... and a perfectly decent skirt ...'

*

The winter of 1943. War. Famine.

Stalin had a dream about Lenin.

In the dream Lenin beckoned Stalin to the window and pointed to the square where the people had gathered. 'Listen Joseph,' said Lenin, 'if you don't give them another hundred grammes of bread a day they'll soon be following me!'

*

It was decided to open a striptease in Moscow's Conference Palace. Submissions were made, permission granted, billboards posted, but not a soul turned up to the first performance.

Next morning there was a call from the Central Committee: 'Why was the undertaking a failure?'

'We've no idea,' replied the organizers. 'It was superbly organized and all the striptease artists had a solid Party record,

---

* Infamous head of the CHEKA or 'secret police' — predecessor to the KGB.

they were Bolsheviks from 1905. Some of them even knew Lenin personally.'

*

'What's new in the shops?'
'One furniture factory has begun production of a three-sleeper bed for newly-weds called "Lenin is with us". And a perfume factory has developed a new scent called "Eau de Lénine".'*

* The literal translation of this is 'Lenin's stream'. One could also, perhaps, translate it 'Lenin piss' . . .

## Comrade Stalin

During the war Lieutenant Ivanov stood on guard by Stalin's study door and as he walked by Stalin would enjoy having a joke with him.

'What, Comrade Ivanov, you haven't been shot yet?'

'No, Comrade Stalin,' Ivanov would reply white-faced and standing stiffly to attention.

Time passed. Ivanov had become a major but as before he stood guard outside Stalin's study and as before Comrade Stalin passing by would have a little joke with him. 'What, Comrade Ivanov, you haven't been shot yet?'

'No, Comrade Stalin,' replied Major Ivanov.

The war ended. It was Victory Day. Comrade Stalin was making a triumphal speech in the Kremlin.

'Our nation has conquered because our nation never despairs, it loves a good joke . . .'

Stalin paused for a moment. He was looking for someone in the auditorium.

'Isn't that right Comrade Ivanov?' he continued turning to a general sitting not far away.

Up jumped General Ivanov, white-faced. 'Absolutely right, Comrade Stalin.'

\*

Stalin decided to test Party members' loyalty. He summoned a Russian, a Ukrainian and a Jew and ordered them to jump from a tenth floor window.

The Russian went to the window, looked down and begged: 'Comrade Stalin, have mercy, I have a family, children . . .'

Stalin flew into a rage: 'Arrest him!' he ordered.

The Ukrainian walked up to the window, looked down and fell on his knees: 'Have mercy, Comrade Stalin, I'm the only breadwinner in the family . . .'

'Arrest him!' ordered Stalin.

The Jew took off his jacket, took off his trousers, took off his watch and handed them all to Stalin. Then he said: 'Please, give these to my wife . . .' and jumped out of the window.

But Stalin had only been joking and there were nets below so the Jew was not smashed to smithereens. In fact, he was brought back to Stalin.

'Good fellow, Comrade Rabinovich,' said Stalin. 'You have proved yourself a devoted Party member and for that you will receive a medal and I shall see that you get a better job. But, let me ask you, what gave you the courage? After all life, no matter what, is very dear to us.'

Rabinovich was touched.

'I'll tell you frankly, Comrade Stalin. Even death is better than this kind of a life.'

\*

In the twenty-first century a journalist is walking around Moscow with a microphone, asking all the passersby: 'Who was Hitler?'

Nobody knows. At last the journalist comes on a decrepit old man with a Ph.D. in history.

'Hitler? Hitler?' the old man recalls with an effort. 'Ah-ah-ah! I remember. He was a petty demagogue in the Stalinist era.'

# *Olympics 1980*

— Who is the outgoing president of the IOC?
— Lord Misha Kalinin.

*

   Carter wrote a letter to Brezhnev in which he warned that if Soviet troops were not withdrawn from Afghanistan, the next Olympiad would also be in Moscow.

*

What are the three stages of the XXII Olympiad?

    1  The long years of preparation
    2  The two short weeks of competition
    3  The renaissance of the people's economy

# Russian Sketches: Drunk and Sober

'Russia cannot be fathomed with the mind.'
*F. I. Tyutchev**

A drunk was standing in the town's main square urinating.
A policeman came up.
'Put that away and stop immediately!' he shouted.
The drunk did up his fly. The policeman walked away and the drunk began roaring with laughter.
'What are you laughing about?' asked another drunk.
'I put it away, but I didn't stop . . .'

\*

A drunk stops a passerby in the street and says: 'Tell me, mate, where is the other side of the street?'

\* Tyutchev was a metaphysical poet of the nineteenth century.

'Over there.' The passerby points across the road.

'Now, lad, don't tell lies.' The drunk gets angry. 'They just sent me here from over there.'

*

A railway station. A whistle blows and a train pulls out. Just at this moment three men rush on to the platform. Seeing the train leaving, they fling themselves after it. The train gathers speed. Two of the men somehow manage to jump on. The third is left behind. He stands on the platform laughing.

'What are you laughing for?' asks a porter.

'The people that came to see me off have caught the train and I've stayed behind . . .'

*

A drunk is dragging himself along the railway sleepers: 'The bastards, what a staircase they've built. It seems to go on for ever and no banisters!'

*

A drunk was sprawled across the border between the town and the country. Up came a policeman who looked at the drunk and then phoned in to police headquarters:

'There's a drunk on the border between the town and the country. Which way should I drag him, to the town station or to the regional?'

'Have a sniff,' says the chief. 'If he reeks of cheap wine, then take him to the regional station. If it's vodka, then into town.'

The policeman had a sniff and reported back:

'Comrade Chief, he smells of cognac.'

'Then don't touch him. Why shouldn't he relax!'

*

A quiet-looking man was standing at a trolley-bus stop. Suddenly he seizes his head in his hands and cries out in despair: 'Oh! Fuck!'

'Comrade, comrade,' the other people at the stop hiss at him. 'Don't forget you're not at home. There are women and children here.'

'I beg your pardon,' says the man and once more becomes absorbed in his own thoughts. About five minutes go by and he again seizes his head in his hands and cries out, 'Oh! Fuck!'

'How dare you!' exclaim the others. 'We'll show you! Where's a policeman . . ?'

Just at that moment a policeman approaches.

'What do you think you're doing, friend? Creating a disturbance? Do you know what you're liable to get for that . . ?'

Apologetically the man leans towards the policeman and whispers something in his ear.

'Oh! Fuck!' exclaims the policeman in an agitated voice.

There is a renewed rumpus among the crowd. 'What on earth is going on?' they shout indignantly.

'Quiet comrades!' shouts the policeman. 'Our friend here has suffered a great tragedy. His wife has given birth to a black baby . . .'

'Oh! Fuck!' wail one and all, clasping their heads between their hands . . .

*

An aesthete walked into a cake shop and ordered a cake in the shape of the Acropolis. The baker took the order and told him to come back in two days' time.

Two days later the aesthete came back.

The baker put the cake in front of him.

'Wonderful, wonderful!' exclaimed the aesthete. 'But there's just one detail that's not quite right. The Acropolis has six steps . . . and you've only got five. That will have to be put right, my friend.'

'Very well,' agreed the baker. 'Come back tomorrow.'

The next day the aesthete was back.

The baker put the cake in front of him.

'Marvellous, marvellous!' raved the aesthete. 'A real work of art . . . Ah-h-h . . . but, there's still a small mistake, my friend. On the Acropolis the eighth pilaster from the left is brown, whereas you've made it yellow . . .'

'Very well,' said the baker, 'come back in an hour and we'll have it right.'

An hour later the aesthete came back.

'Ah, now that's made all the difference,' he gushed. 'Everything is just right. A real facsimile. Excellent. Wonderful! Thank you, my friend, you've made me so happy . . .'

'Shall I wrap it for you?' asked the baker.

'No need, my friend, no need.' The aesthete waved him away. 'I'm going to eat it right now.'

\*

A provincial is returning home after a trip to Moscow. His friends are full of questions:

'Well, what's it like in the capital. It must be real good, eh?'

'Oh, yes, very good,' says the provincial. 'Very, very good.'

'I bet you went everywhere, eh?'

'Everywhere,' replies the provincial.

'Did you go to the Bolshoi too, eh?'

'I did,' replies the provincial.

'Well, and what was it like, good?'

'Very good . . . So warm . .'

\*

An intellectual goes up to the box office in a theatre.

'Two seats in the front row, please,' he says to the cashier.

'There are no seats left,' she replies.

'What do you mean!' says the intellectual. 'I only need two tickets.'

'But I haven't even got one,' she replies.

'Try and understand,' he fusses, 'I cannot possibly miss this première. I am an intellectual. I come to all your premières. For me to miss one is unthinkable. You just must understand that without the theatre life for an intellectual would not be worth living . . .'

The intellectual's wife tugs at his coat from behind: 'Let's forget it . . .' she says.

The intellectual turns to his wife: 'Get fucked, you bitch!'

Turning back to the box office: 'As I was saying . . .'

\*

1943. Snowbound Moscow. A fierce frost. Churchill is walking down Gorky Street. Coming towards him is a peasant, his sheepskin coat wide open, his jacket unbuttoned, his shirt undone. The peasant is scratching his bare chest and eating ice cream.

Churchill stops stunned: 'No one will ever be able to beat these people!'

*

'Yes, we are Scythians! Yes, we are Asiatics!'
*Alexander Blok**

* Alexander Blok was a symbolist poet of the early years of this century.

# The Unforgettable Hero of The Civil War, Vasilii Ivanovich Chapaev and His Faithful Orderly Petka

Petka, the orderly, asked Vasilii Ivanovich Chapaev: 'Vasilii Ivanovich, have you ever really loved?'

'Yes, I've loved, Petka,' sighed Vasilii Ivanovich.

'What was it like?' Petka asked undeterred.

'Well, what can I say . . ?' Vasilii Ivanovich sighed once more. 'I had to shoot it. It went lame in the rear left leg . . .'

\*

\* These characters are heroes of the civil war (1918-21) well-known to Soviet audiences from their portrayal in countless novels, plays, operas and films. Here they are treated with rather less than the usual respect.

Vasilii Ivanovich is teaching Petka how to use a hand grenade.

'This is what you do, Petka. You take the grenade in your right hand. With your left hand you pull the ring. And when the bastard hisses, you throw it. Did you get that?'

Petka nods enthusiastically.

'Excellent!' Then, let's see you do it,' says Vasilii Ivanovich, getting well out of the way, just in case.

Petka takes the grenade in his right hand, pulls the ring with his left, listens for a few seconds until it hisses then spins around and shouts: 'Vasilii Ivanovich! Catch!'

\*

Petka is trying to write an essay for a literature class. He sits there racking his brains.

'What's making you so miserable?' asks Vasilii Ivanovich.

'I have to write this essay on 'What I did yesterday'.

'Well, and what did you do?'

'The same as every other day! I drank!'

'What an idiot you are, Petka,' says Vasilii Ivanovich.

'You can't write that. Go through the essay and every time you come to the word "drank", put "read" instead. Then it will sound a lot more cultured.'

Petka is thrilled and begins to scratch away: 'I got up yesterday morning and read half a book. I thought for a moment and read the other half. It didn't seem like enough, so I set off to the shop for another book. On the way I saw Vasilii Ivanovich coming towards me . . . and his eyes were so well read . . .'

\*

Vasilii Ivanovich is standing in the main street lazily chewing away. Up comes Petka.

'What are you doing, Vasilii Ivanovich?'

'Nothing much, Petka. As you can see I am hanging around like a hippy . . .'

'What are you chewing, Vasilii Ivanovich? Did you get some American chewing gum from somewhere?'

'Good heavens no, I'm washing my socks . . .'

# *This Is Radio Armenia!*

Exact Armenian time is six, seven or nearly eight!

## *The Next Programme is 'The Armenian Alphabet' You ask — we have an Answer!*

*Citizen A from City B asks:*
Why did the rooster peck the hen's head as he mounted her?
*Our Reply:* So she wouldn't think he wanted to marry her!

*Citizen B from City C asks:*
If everything is going so well in the country, then why are things so bad?
*Our Reply:* That's the dialectical unity of opposites.

*Citizen C from City D asks:*
What is the most common cause of death?
*Our Reply:* Life.

*Citizen D from City E asks:*
   What's the difference between a knight and a maiden?
*Our Reply:*   The knight fights to the last drop of blood, the maiden to the first.

*Citizen E from City F asks:*
   What's a pessimist?
*Our Reply:*   A man to whom an optimist owes money.

*Citizen F from City G asks:*
   What's abortion?
*Our Reply:*   Capital punishment without trial.

*Citizen G from City H asks:*
   What is a point of view?
*Our Reply:*   When a man's horizons narrow to a point, he calls that point his point of view.

*Citizen H from City I asks:*
   What should the fireman do when the train is coming up to a crooked stretch of line?
*Our Reply:*   Throw crooked logs in the fire box.

*Citizen I from City K asks:*
   How can I stop the hair falling out of my gorgette?
*Our Reply:*   We don't know what a gorgette is, but if it's what we think it is, we advise you to give up cycling.

*Citizen K from City L asks:*
   Can you sit bare-arse on a hedgehog?
*Our Reply:*   Yes, on two conditions: a) if you shave the hedgehog, or b) if it's not your arse.

*Citizen L from City M asks:*
   Why aren't women accepted into the army?
*Our Reply:* Because of the way they obey the order 'Lie Down!'


*Citizen M from City N asks:*
   How can you tell a person from Odessa?
*Our Reply:* A sailor's chest. A stevedore's back. A footballer's arse.


*Citizen N from City O asks:*
   Is it possible to buy a priceless object?
*Our Reply:* No, but you can steal one.


*Citizen O from City P asks:*
   Is it possible to deceive someone who trusts you?
*Our Reply:* How can you deceive someone who doesn't trust you?


*Citizen P from City Q asks:*
   What's the difference between a man and a woman?
*Our Reply:* A man always wants it, but can't always do it, and a woman can always do it, but doesn't always want it.


*Citizen Q from City R sends us a riddle:*
   Name a short word which rouses women, which our people love and little boys write on lavatory walls!
*Our Reply:* The Party!


*Citizen R from City S asks:*
   What's an instant cure for smokers?
*Our Reply:* Light the cigarette at both ends!

*Citizen S from City T asks:*
  Should one quarrel with the management?
*Our Reply:*   Quarrelling with the management is like pissing
  against the wind.


*Citizen T from City U writes:*
  I want to marry the daughter of very old-fashioned parents.
  Is it all right to ask for her hand?
*Our Reply:*   Why just her hand?


*Citizen U from City V asks:*
  What can you bring back from a trip abroad without having
  to worry about Soviet customs?
*Our Reply:*   Sweet memories.


*Citizen V from City W asks:*
  What can you do, when the large bosom goes out of fashion?
*Our Reply:*   Wear it out.


*Citizen W from City X asks:*
  Who qualifies for the name of 'gentleman' these days?
*Our Reply:*   The man who takes the lighted cigarette out of his
  mouth when he kisses a lady's hand.


*Citizen X from City Y asks:*
  How can I get rid of the crabs?
*Our Reply:*   There are two methods: *Method One* Hang a half-
  hundred weight on your balls. The crabs will die laughing.
  *Method Two* Take off your pants and sit on some salt-
  herring. The crabs will make a meal of the salt-herring and
  be overcome by a terrible thirst. Then go down to the seaside
  and sit on the sand. The crabs will rush down to the water,
  and you should piss off.

*Citizen Y from City Z asks:*
 What should you eat on board ship during a storm?
*Our Reply:*  The cheapest thing on the menu.


*Citizen Z from City . . . (unspecified) asks:*
 Why can a fart in the kitchen be heard in the dining room?
*Our Reply:*  Stupid questions go unanswered.